Journeying from Canyon de Chelly

Journeying from Canyon de Chelly

Poems by Catharine Savage Brosman

Louisiana State University Press

Baton Rouge and London

1990

Copyright © 1972, 1973, 1974, 1976, 1977, 1978, 1980, 1982, 1983, 1984,
1985, 1986, 1987, 1988, 1989, 1990 by Catharine Savage Brosman
All rights reserved
Manufactured in the United States of America
First printing

99 98 97 96 95 94 93 92 91 90   5 4 3 2 1

Designer: Albert Crochet
Typeface: Linotron Trump Mediaeval
Typesetter: The Composing Room of Michigan, Inc.
Printer and binder: Thomson-Shore, Inc.

LIBRARY OF CONGRESS CATALOGING-IN-PUBLICATION DATA

Brosman, Catharine Savage, date.
    Journeying from Canyon de Chelly : poems / by Catharine Savage
Brosman.
        p.   cm.
    ISBN 0-8071-1626-2 (alk. paper). — ISBN 0-8071-1627-0 (alk. paper
: pbk.)
    I. Title.
PS3552.R666J68   1990
811'.54—dc20   90-33362
                                                        CIP

The author offers grateful acknowledgment to the editors of the following
publications, in which poems in this book originally appeared: Claflin
Review, "Tres Hermanas," "At the Museum: Women and Men,"
"Watching Bees"; Georgia Review, "Eating Pears at Midnight"; Interim,
"Chaco Canyon: The Fire," "Driving to Vézelay," "Apples"; Louisiana
Literature, "Letter to R. W.," "Islands," "Magpies," "Buck Moths";
Sewanee Review, "Vézelay, II: The Basilica," "Reading Old Letters,"
"Cleaning the Shed," "Birds at Night," "Peaches"; Shenandoah, "Spring
Raking"; Slant, "Lazarus"; South Dakota Review, "Vézelay, I"; Southern
Humanities Review, "Landscape with Peasants"; Southern Poetry Review,
"Wires"; Southern Review, "Journeying from Canyon de Chelly,"
"Crossing to Evian," "Falling at Mont-Saint-Michel," "Woman in Red:
Vogue Cover, 1919," "Note Left on the Front Table, 1940," "The Blinded
Man at Night," "Ash Lawn," "Liberty Furnace," "The Loft," "Clear
Creek," "Windmills," "History," "Route 29," "Assateague in Winter,"
"Abiding Winter," "Augusta County: Perspectives in Snow,"
"Strawberries," "Grass," "Crows," "Destin: Swimming on Easter Day";
Texas Quarterly, "Notes from a Reconstruction"; Xavier Review,
"Variations at Pass Christian." "Eating Pears at Midnight" also appeared
as the third-place poem in Best Poems of 1973 (Palo Alto, Calif., 1974);
"Route 29," "Cleaning the Shed," and "Crows" appeared in the Anthology
of Magazine Verse (Beverly Hills, Calif., 1981, 1984, 1987).

Publication of this book has been supported by a grant from the
National Endowment for the Arts in Washington, D.C., a federal agency.

The paper in this book meets the guidelines for permanence and
durability of the Committee on Production Guidelines for Book Longevity
of the Council on Library Resources. ⊗

In memory of my father: measure and light

Contents

Journeying from Canyon de Chelly

Journeying from Canyon de Chelly

i

Motions intact through the morning, below
complacent clouds, and light multiplying
its beneficence, emulate the undulations
of the mind. There's method in outdistancing
these mesas, which darken to uncertainty:
ahead, the lucid air in variations shapes
its pleasures as a piñoned range, impressed
on mere mirages of the blue. Stillness
matures. The pure idea of desert walks,
phantasmally, upon immense and soundless
sands. The salmon mallow waves, and hawks
deploy their purpose on indifferent winds.

ii

Solicitations from the crest prevailed.
This *is* a change—lunch among the trees,
a dark reflection, eyelids closed, before
the tremors of descent. A cautious light
anticipates commotions. In the juniper,
the singing ceases. What can we confirm
of dream—except the shadowy murmuring,
the swift lactescent stream and figures
dying on the water's face—if past the far
plateaus, the streaking sky ignites, then
breaks toward storm and strafes a ridge,
vaunting its modulations of the visible?

iii

What was proposed in ecstasies of clouds
and later, vast illuminations only seems
transcendent, trumpeting glory; the light
consumes itself, without desire. At dusk,
images flush up on radiant wings, and fill
the air with cries from distant flights.
Another journey follows, like remembering
the cottonwoods along the San Juan River
where we camped that night—no moon at all,
the willows stirring, heavy in the wake
of rain, and the current swelling, resonant
and strange, as in the plenitude of thought.

Betatakin

To find—perhaps then later to be found—
we left our mesa brothers, and have come,
o Father World, to this place, at the end
of canyons, where the piñon thicket, dense
as hair, proposes berries, fruit, and birds

abundant. The cave is smooth and resonant
as calabash; from rim to rim, each sound
rings clear, and sunlight, reaching from
the farther cliff at dawn, embraces stone.
Like deer, we summer now, without a hearth;

but the pile of timbers rises every day;
we shape the stone to purpose, as a word
intends an act; and when the vault is done,
in kiva darkness we will name the ground,
then breathe on dormant grain, to plant

the corn of winter's care. The elders say
that we are in the upper sphere, the third
division of a sacred circle, like the sun,
that carries us; only the last, when earth
herself is harvested, remains. The wheel

is turning. I the artist write with bone
on rock the rings of time that will reveal
to strangers even our designs. Gods, lend
them eyes within to know to what immense
and latter end their labors must be bound.

Chaco Canyon: The Fire

After the spark, piñon needles
fan into light, then in its power
shrivel to wisps, yielding
to the crackling boughs,
the eloquence of sage. An old

lover, evening wind, hovers
at the edges, touching off the fire
of the blood, shaping
to its desires the hydra flames,
which flay about, embracing

to devour. Their singing plays
like shadows over thought. Toppling
in the conflagration
to the west, a city of clouds
smolders to ruins. Summer's

greenest memory is now consumed,
while running at the core,
the winy resin sputters. Fingers
of smoke dissolve
into the darkness. Truly,

we are here, below the canyon rim,
sentient and free, the mind
burning with its own heat.
From the coals, ashes
form, falling among the stones.

Chaco Canyon: The Ruins

The sun burst, swollen, every dawn,
seared its way across a molten sky,
smoldered late and burnt the image
of its flames in the gnawing dreams
of the Anasazi. Another granary
was emptied as the beast of drought
devoured the grass. When the raven

left, driven by memories of green,
the Anasazi followed, extinguishing
their kiva's sacred fires, grieving
for ritual words that had resounded
from the rocks, where painted bodies
bled, empowering the hunter's spear,
and totem birds like angels hovered.

Now the summer's hands are reaping
light, and from the shadows, blue
awakens, shapes the mesa, mingling
among the sage. Already strangers
measure differences. If you stand
where the rays of the solstice sun
fall from the compass of the world

and pierce the ruined nave to mark
the north, you see the many rooms
of another mind. The futile stones
have settled like a grave. Beside
the cliffs, rank with guano, canyon
wrens are circling by their nests;
in the distance, dust and exile stir.

Tres Hermanas

Ramona Tenorio, have you heard
what these hills mean, marking the road
to Las Palomas—
three cupolas (put bells in them
and the desert will ring)

or the cusps of history
(Pancho Villa came across right here,
the evening of his raid);
or do they promise offerings of love
(bird's-egg beads you shaped,

turquoise and obsidian, hang now
on my breast)? You listen
at your pueblo door, under cottonwood
beams, your dark, defiant hair
above a face cracking like adobe,

hands hovering over
hosts of silver; your ancestors' gods
are hammered in your legends,
where all their children join them,
strung on silence. The doves

do not sing. These barren slopes,
piñon-pocked arroyos,
bear our names (Tres Hermanas, Animas,
Victorio) as if we belonged
to the house of the world, though

the sky by day burns hard as quartz
above our shadows, and tonight
the moon will sharpen spears of agave
before they bloom to death,
crowned in coral white. The beads say,

You live on visions, flickering
as in a hermitage,
minds caught in things' metamorphoses—
no congruence, no voice;
only the strange mothering of stones.

Crossing to Evian

There's the dock, clearing the water's blue
and vibrant eye. Quickly! A ticket; two
steps; and we are slicing floes of spray
toward the Alps. No shade on deck; the sun
is hammering the waves to steel. The wind,

the liquid warmth, a white and weightless
bird tracing his line, reveal nothing, only
their own sufficiency, as though—suspending
recognition—we were strangers to the world;
and the resounding sunlight splashes across

the lake—until the shadows banked ahead
become the stern, ascending wall of peaks,
and the shapes of trees and terraced stone
begin to signify the shore. Later, friends
will ask us for accounts, supposing that

we bring back something neat and telling,
like a photograph; but have you tried to fit
a glimpse of order, knowing and perfected
in its resplendent gaze, into the journey's
darkness, the moving contours of the mind?

Falling at Mont-Saint-Michel

Rising tide. Between the saline meadows:
the dike—the road—and wind, ferreting
everywhere. On the dunes, poppies bend
in clusters, flagging the way (this is
June), and sheep crop the bitter grass,

flavoring their flesh. The holy mountain,
braced and walled, appears to meditate—
a friar in his cell, gargoyles sunning—
but a path ropes up, leaving you panting,
into its recesses. By the abbey church,

a garden dozes. Imagination wanders past
the parapets, but the body's certainty
inhabits rock. All around, the clouds,
the sands are churning; the Norman coast
is heaving in an avalanche of waves. If

you toss a pebble down, it plunges, dips,
taking your eye; but throw a word: *sea*,
its ripples are invisible; does it tell
the ocean's flashing music, or what throbs
in its stream? Plovers dive, and a feel

of wings deceives you, as if leaping were
to capture light in motion, to become
the bird of knowledge—and not to fall,
descending to a darkness where the surf
itself is silent as the heart of stone.

Windmills by Saint-Malo

Too much water on the coast! It washed
the road, embroiled the skies in mist—
or was it winnowed rain?—so one might
miss a turn, or founder in the distances
between prevision and the actual; still,
imagination's shapes appeared as menhirs

harboring among the bells their ancient
deities, and windmills, mushroom-brown,
at work like egrets in the saline marsh.
So much strangeness in an unaccustomed
scene! Such strangeness in accustomed
selves! At last, the mass of turbulence

tore into a clearing; rippled cloudbanks
moved as to the open sea. To sail behind
the squall, hightailing it—its breath
still wet—were another vision, had not
the rinsed and layered light collapsed
in folds, releasing distant lamps. Is this

what one desires, to confirm that even
here, the day is swallowed by the moment,
letting us declare the mind's dominion
beyond the old and turning world? What
matters surely isn't just a rounded moon
teasing the sea, a dinner with a foreign

flavor! Walking the parapets at night,
we followed two old women, earthen-faced,
sharpening their silence on the stones,
perhaps remembering their mother's eyes,
as calls of seabirds drifted, answering
the slacking tide. Like Titans harrowing

the darkness for their children's bread,
the windmills whirled their widow arms
and gestured toward the moon, to signify,
"We are the witnesses of earth and sea,
the daughters of the moments you invoke,
who watch the passing waters, and survive."

Driving to Vézelay

The road uncoils, deliberating, silent
and austere between the cairns. Along
the fields, the stubble weathers; reeds
and russet ferns in coveys flush beside
the ponds. What mirrors friends of many
years also fits the mind, its soundings

keener in the steady light of winter's
cell. Beyond a screen of firs, a steeple
miters the horizon; later, choirs of trees
are vested in a hasty snow. By evening,
we ascend the buttressed mountain, turning
up beside the great facade. The valley

falls away on either side, revealing its
designs. A visit next, our voices belling
in the cold. The discourse of our selves
has been unrest, and quarrels with those
we loved—such crossing lines belying
clarity—as Magdalene lay with many men,

until the Teacher moved her with divine
desire. She wept, then, over his shroud.
Here, the body of her faith rises in arch
and tower. Our acts are stones, quarried
from the darkest earth, in conflict hewn,
before the reconciling walls are built.

Vézelay, I

For Jules Roy

Approaching it is all a matter
of point of view. You can be following
a little valley road,
twisting around fields
in a lazy summer fog; suddenly,
it commands you, and the valley,
pulling your eyes
to the summit. Later, if
you arrive on foot, barely matching

the wind, you will climb
between the blinders of rough
houses, each one shouldering the next.
Perhaps you meet a couple
of old women, shawled in black,
or, at vespers,
monks fluttering like sparrows
as they gather in the square.
The facade engages every glance—

a fortress, flanked
and turreted and buttressed, still
in sunlight when the alleys
have been overcome
by dark. Nothing but a terrace
here, and the heavens, for a horizon;
but you sense the weight
of rock hauled up the slope,
the pulley chafing, hands

and chisels at their sacramental
tasks. Viollet-le-Duc
saw the church as ruined patrimony,
worn down like the faith
it had made substantial,
and shored it up, timbers and hull
and bow. The lintel's length,
statues, scourged by time, like tortured
bodies seem to endure again

the evil of the age,
while on the tympanum, the saints
conversing, opening their books,
in wonder gesture toward
the seated Christ,

in fluid robes, his radiant hands
a sign of fire to come; the dark sea
of his eyes profound,
searching from within the stone.

Vézelay, II: The Basilica

Darkness.
Beyond the narthex,
space, swelling
as the eyes hew out the nave.
A fugue of pillars,
and then the leap of arches,
vaulting to a single chord.

Clusters of caned chairs,
squat as if for children, give
the body's measure.
The mind fills out the rest,
transepts and apse,
the hull full sail.
Casting a honeyed light,

islands of votive lamps
reveal the grain of slabs
and columns. This basilica
belongs to Magdalene
of the double life, whose bones
became the leaven of belief,
that raised up stone

like bread. In the crypt,
her reliquary almost beats—
a heart concealed
in a great body;
but the recesses are cold
and shadowy, the way
the tomb appeared to her,

in the chary dawn,
its portal opened; and she,
sleepless, not finding
what she expected,
turned in tears to inquire
of the gardener, already
silently about his chores.

Woman in Red: *Vogue* Cover, 1919

i

Everything about the war
(the officers, benumbed, and remnants
of men demobilized at last,
returning from the charnel house,
leaving the soil of Picardy
festering with limbs and iron),
everything appears denied
by her Beardsley throat, the parchment
and bamboo of a parasol,
the harmony of almond eyes
and hands. Full as the lilies
on her broad-brimmed hat,
like lovers' parted lips,
heavy blossoms on her dress
magnify in red the flowering
of early summer. Sounds of parties
linger still among the swirls—
laughter, and the tune of innocence
to be replayed, after the frenzy
at the slaughtering stone.

ii

She, and the flowers,
seem out of time,
because they were so much of it—
not just a flame of summer, quick
as the expressions of the sea,
and pressed upon the memory,
but the long sickness of the war
brilliantly relieved
for a moment in her dress,
after the exploding blood
of Mametz Wood, Verdun. She looks
indifferent, but in her eyes
is mirrored the remembrance of the men
who lived on images
(gardens rimmed by privet
hedge, linen and clean hands,
the sweet, uncluttered air)
and celebrated women in their minds,
which turn flesh
into the form of the ideal.

iii

Since, she has given her hand
to time, joining the despoiled
whose names garland the village steles,
the stone of common naves.
Let those whose ritual
was the daily reckoning of the dead
remind us: "When the bloodthirsty beast
who has defined the lark
that sang at morning, heralding
the guns, and can admire
the dolmen cliffs of France, serene
above the spray,
has finished killing its own kind,
they will have died twice—
the woman in red,
the woman you love most and bend over
gravely to embrace tonight—
even the image gone,
and in these fields, nothing left
for God to reap save shards."

Note Left on the Front Table, 1940

What we said today was not enough. You know
how music rises from the darkness of the mind,
then vanishes—and something not revealed
before has taken shape. Can you comprehend
how difference is a mirror? Yet in your pain
leaving pains me, Mother. What you have done

for me would keep any man, if love could mend
character and circumstance.—Now, thrifty birds
garner the dusk; an owl calls, across a field;
the answer is repeated, like a furtive light
that flickers on the river's brow. As though
a tree of dreams were budding in me, blind,

I hear a rustling of brilliant wings. Strange:
at close to forty, failure is the other face
of strength: I shall not lend to money my one
life, like other men, nor mutilate my words
in rhetoric. Or does the worm of cowardice
possess me? Well, we shall see: the war is

not yet ours, but will be soon; I cannot bend,
but can make my body serve. If there is grace
enough for us, then afterwards, I shall write
better to you, as I make peace in the moraine
of myself, winnowing the thoughts that blow
through leaves of light along a verdant range.

Lazarus

The witnesses—so fixed upon the figure
who, moved by a flood of tears,
bade Lazarus arise, astonished,
from his stony berth, like a bird
flushed up—left him alone then
with his sisters, despite the amazement,
to follow the one whose hands

bestowed the life their words
could only imitate. Afterwards, to be
once more a thing extended, feel
the familiar flesh within and out,
and suffer till he died again—
it is not known if Lazarus complained,
nor if he remembered passing,

shaken, by the strand
where shapes of the forlorn contorted
in the bleeding trees; then
hesitating, when the healer's voice
summoned him back, as he reached
the other shore—the flocks of hills
browsing in plenty, angels

stirring, as they might
when evening breaks along the southern
range, the sagebrush pungent
as a holy perfume, and a blue
so royal, pinned by the early stars,
that wings release the mind
and lift it to the very gates of God.

The Blinded Man at Night

The day is voices still, commotions,
wind; the night, an absence. Only
in my mind are the stars gathering,
swinging into place their choruses,
but without music. What used to sing
to me in their circling—leaves alive
and blowing on the tree of darkness
—was the connection. All distance

and awesome burning, those heavens!
yet they were refreshing to the eyes,
a stream spilling down familiar pines.
As though others, too, were blinded,
words no longer bear their offering
of light. Somewhere, tongues of fire
may teach the dead to read the signs
again, to see as angels; but I do not

speak their language, yet. If I ask
the animals who forage in my dreams,
among a field of stars, they reply
that they know little of the world,
except the ache arising in the loins,
which drives them out, their muzzle
trembling, their eyes aflame. I rub
my lids, the lintel of my brow. What

shaft, even of pain, will ever reach
as deep as light? I can remember it
inside, corollas bursting as of blood,
and on my forehead, pure and palpable
like rain. My hands caress the dark,
its silent waves, its ring of sightless
dust: I shall be mute, beyond crying,
burnt to the inner essence of a man.

At the Museum: Women and Men

i Passion

While a shrouded mourner turns away
from what should not bear watching
by the rest of us, the mother faces
the shame—not even throwing herself
on the earth, foreign now with neither
the emblematic beasts, nor the warmth
of straw. Stabat mater cum pendente
filius. The scene, painted in piety,
has become a lesson in perspective.
Is it because salvation seems remote
that this altarpiece signifies mere
style? From the signs, ours appears
a time for further crucifixions; even
then, despite the star, the portents
were not good: violence and vicious
governors, one of whom had children
murdered at the breast, foreseeing veils
that would descend like thunderbolts.

ii Portraits

They tell everything about themselves,
the pain, the knowledge (Rembrandt's
eyes, seeing in both directions); most
of all, the pride which starches souls,
precise as Hals's burghers, whose lace
and embonpoint measured their wealth,
while half of Europe burnt. Sometimes
they sing to us: the Renoirs, a Manet,
the girls of Morisot; others terrify,
the way the grandees of Velázquez hurl
authority like a spear, and Hapsburg
rulers curl their lip, or a reveler
smiles madly in his lust. In Van Gogh's
stare, the splendor of a starry night
is hidden in his granite gaze or haloed
in a bandage, to remind us of desire, aching
for an absence, like the mutilated ear.

iii Café

That woman over there, sitting alone:
all morning, she studied the pictures,
taking notes (when she brushed past,
the last time, she barely smiled); now
she finishes her salad indifferently,
as if remembering the apples of Cézanne
with their robust shine, or a peeled
lemon by a carafe, in Chardin's light.
She has the distant look of paintings,
yet she is familiar, a mirrored face,
where the traces of reflection pass,
flickering, as on a river in the wind.
Beneath the surface, something elusive
moves, a darkness apprehension cannot
reach, but which cries, dances, leaps
from the canvases, drawing the mind by
images—the self to the second power,
the dreamlike explication of a dream.

Ash Lawn

December. Where a cold sun glazed the snow,
and left the lanes to ice,
Ash Lawn waits out another year.
It lasts unrestored, uncluttered
by costumed ladies, craftsmen in buckled shoes
selling tourist wares; a single housekeeper
is nearly idle, leading no one else
through the narrow rooms
of Monroe's house, or his more ample mind
reflected by trees opening on
a prospect of hills. In this late time,

what is left? Without
fires burning, sheets under the counterpane,
there is no reality in the beds,
no virtue in the sideboard tureens;
nothing lives except intruders' breath
and, outside, the boxwood,
slow, seasonless green.
Might not one remain at home, warmer,
and know just as well there the loneliness
of things abandoned?

To hear an echo of oneself, or survive
among designs outlived, one should not need
history. What brings us here is worse:
not architectural grace, beauty of ornament
or line, nor the incidental picturesque
that makes us say, "Well, this is different,"
but death—
keener, finer than in our own mirror.

In spring, years later, I still look back on it,
not touching bottom anywhere.

Liberty Furnace

Yet we had thought about it before:
narrow lives back in those hollows,
faces born to plain rail fences—a web
of years, white with love's moons,
the snows, the buried child; then all
become twice past, in a rush of vines
and vindicated ash, that greened
even death.

        Reaching the cul-de-sac,
dropped between cat's cradle ribs,
one came into exile, met wildness
riding down the pits, endured its roar
—a struggling of winds, an animal
gasp—unless it were ghosts who cried
from the ridge's throat.

        But this
hardness was liberty; or so they named
the forge; and the streams ran red
for a hundred years with Allegheny
iron and a hammered strength, until
the weathercock hung askew, pointing
toward loss, all loss.

        What wounds
autumn now leaves on these hills,
which no mill can wash; flames leap
down from the sun, the brick turns
incandescent, and fire burns again,
to refine our late indifference,
before our bones shall blanch

        like theirs
below the willows; not that we should ever
make our bread, our staves from this
soil, but ask the question always: Can
we live more freely with their iron
in our heart, this side of their peace?

The Loft

i

Do you remember coming up the steps,
narrow as a ship's ladder,
to the loft, summer evenings?
Along the fence, hydrangeas lifted
toward the damp sky their litmus blue;
a mimosa wind made the curtains
float like nightgowns.
As light hovered in a moon above the lamp,
the house moved under way toward night,
to the music of birds
and of love. The hours ran deep;
they might have been immobile.

ii

Crossing night so often since, without
you, I have thought back
on the garden, stirring, and light
almost green. Later, after the surprise
of parting, my mind remained in that room
with its polished ship's wood
and prospect over the trees,
and told directions by its coordinates,
believing not untruth but the unseen,
as gnats undulate invisible
on streams of air,
circling evening in a nebula.

iii

Tonight the moon crests high, and pines
toss their riggings; two birds
talk late. This time with you again
recalls a long dusk, and then the wind
fills the sails of the trees
and we run free. It is as if to love
were to look two ways, fullest
on the swell of the remembered laugh,
a place familiar; yet changing,
like clouds moving on the turning air,
as we watched them from the loft,
in diversity of flight.

Reading Old Letters

These are the letters I did not burn—
always saving something, even ruins,
or what appeared to be. One never
knows what will survive, what words,
what loves. Lines streak across
my mind the way rain slants against
a pane, betokening a whole storm.
Perhaps poring over palimpsests,
or tablets from a digging, might
have readied one for this—except
it is myself that I am reading, seen
through the lenses of the others,
a layer covered up but never quite
forgotten; and I grow backwards into
knowledge, seeing blindness, catching
in white scraps the shape of what was,
and how the cryptic present needs
what is to come. Memory flashes on,
then blows itself out. Afterwards,
I write these lines, like another,
obscure letter—in ignorance again.

Notes from a Reconstruction

i

It can come simply—fingers of light
reaching into sleep—and then darkness
slips among the stones. Has my mind
ever been distant from this moment,
imagining already in its dream a day
smooth as a still cove, eyes without
tears, more brilliant than before?

ii

You had leaned there so often, the sea
in your eyes, beside the folded wings
of the dunes. Now, dried sea oats bend
in glass, and your hand brushes mine,
as if we were back at the shore, sails
spread wide to the wind in flight,
where the mending water washes us both.

iii

In the even days of March, the dogwood
is white with stars; woodchucks nose
out, and deer browse among blue thickets
of cabbage palm. What I missed most,
after you, was love's order, that music
as of shoots crossing splashes of sun,
or night dipping toward our piny bed.

iv

There by the bridge, water as green
as the marsh grass still reaches down
the Sound. By your side, the ache
of all this time spent apart breaks
with the waves, and falls; I think
how loving passes loss, while birds
wheel wide, calling above their nests.

Letter to R. W.

Old friend, since you have written about me
(among all the women who were your passion),
something of us both has become historical
now. Have you observed how a poem, public
even when discreet, usually professes more
than one's private words without measure—
than you said on those spring evenings when,

drunk with the blue dream of the Shenandoah,
we followed nightfall down to your cottage,
and over our glasses of Virginia Gentleman
tried to make a rough poetics come together
from the disorder of our life. Good critics,
both—good at the distinctions of the mind.
Your dog would twitch and whimper, sleeping

on its mystery; moths, sallying to the lamp,
hooked back along the beams, working recesses
where the smoke dissolved in darkness. Well,
we were too much like our generation, turning
around alternatives. Such was our lucidity.
Now you judge yourself—a certain sign of age,
and your poem struggles with the unexpressed

(the crude words meaning not less, but more).
What comes to mind, rereading, is an inlet
you picked out that summer, where the water
rippled like spring wheat; umbrella pines
thatching the marsh, and your sun-reddened
beard mingling with my dark and loosened hair.
Reflecting on the uses of carnality, I can say

this for us at least: not power, that jackal,
but self-knowledge, a wiser beast. What little
we have learned began with an embrace: only
afterwards do we confess ourselves as bound
irreconcilably to flesh, the way we understood
the crying of the egrets, gathering at dusk
above the reeds, captives of changeless rites.

Clear Creek

The cold light falls
without indulgence; ravines vein
the slopes; even the rocks
are spare, among the snow. Underneath,
the springs are filling,
but the creek is stone-still.
Though any gesture toward knowing
is uncertain, perhaps
in this hardness, all flux quieted,

something will yield: crust
breaking in a shaft of sun,
the recognition coming. Between
the peaks, sharp pickets
pulling the sky taut,
and the empty road that turns
sinuously as dreams, I scan the circle
of myself. How does one move beyond
the reflected light? If this—

the contours mirror-bright,
the sleeping stream—
if this is someone's history,
there is no vantage point,
as though searching itself obscured
the vision, and clarity
were an illusionist. Mind
remains strange. Here, then, opens
neither the passage through,

the way of seeing from the other side;
all we can hope for
to bring us to the center,
is seepage through time,
at the edge of winter's grave,
and the thin connecting thread
of love. The snow glints,
white on white, like glass;
going down, it will be dark again.

Wires

i

They must be down again, drowned
by the high spring creeks or lying
voiceless in the wind; I call over
the mountain once more, but hear
only the immense space of my heart.

ii

If the storm will not stop soon,
what of the quarrel still live,
the promise halted in midbreath—
are they still hanging somewhere,
debris of love among the shards?

iii

I ring again: nothing comes back,
as if I were calling beyond time,
years out of touch; perhaps air
itself is torn apart; my alien
words have fallen like dead birds.

iv

We are distance, and frenzied to
reach; the wires of my body burn,
ready to snap from pain of being
separate, the desires that stream
sharp and poignant as the stars.

Windmills

Twenty-five miles below Marfa,
we take the ranch road, heading
southeast. The sunlight is pure
but heavy; pools of heat collect
ahead. In the car, a curtain
of brooding hangs between us;
yet, year after year, we find
no other way to go, than to follow
the road of miscontent, bringing
even here our nettles, our pride.

Beside lie agave flats, so spare
of green that even goats graze
there rarely; sand boils and swirls
into a funnel; a dozen Herefords
are foraging on the slope beyond.
I marvel at the lasting habit
of marriage; in ennui's expanse,
our differences are dust storms,
filling the air, grating the skin
and drying the range of the heart.

Now we turn off to dirt tracks
for the jolting climb to the ranch,
the cottonwoods, the shade of stone.
My lips are cracked as soil baked
in a creek bottom. Down a draw,
past desert walnut, and then up
the rough caliche ruts, finally
the first windmill rises, cattle
clustered at the trough; another;
a smoothing of ride over grass.

At the ranch house, we get out
into the hot wind. Nothing more
has been said, and nothing changes
in this vastness where life turns
charily, in circles in the air;
but I find at least a sweet reprieve,
the cool side of the tank, water
pumped from deep wells, drawing
our faces close, and reflecting
the wide pastures of sky behind.

Cleaning the Shed

Something should be done to show out
the old year; inside, work aplenty
waits, or one could celebrate with
an early cheer the sense of change;
but I must look in at what remains
of the year's promises to myself.
Newspapers overflow that old crock,
better fit for moonshine; half-filled
with dirt, pots and jars line a rack;
webby marks on the single pane trace
last summer's spiders. For weeks,
I have walked in a net of broken toys,
fallen rakes and brooms, and watched
the sun's motions grow short; now
in the declining afternoon, little time
is left. This is no domestic rage,
no charade to please the neighbors,
but a gesture to myself, reminding me
of the liens on us, less possessing
than possessed, unless we learn how
to jettison what is outworn. Around
the door, the wind stirs, scattering
twigs from the cedar; birds sort through
the rest of fall. I will pour out
the soil for new worms, cart the trash
for burning, discard the impediments
to plain steps, and clear a few shelves
in my mind—needing to deny Mammon
in at least one way before its trap
consumes me, and make a spot for new
growth, waking in the earth's bones.

Spring Raking

Crackling live oak leaves, fallen
at the full crest of spring, cover
unseasonably the garden's greening,
as on the branch the new growth
pushes, impatient, and the pollen
sails—a promise of giants. Plain
as dust they pile up, these dried
teardrops, but the hybrid trees
yearly bear seedlings in my lawn
with the noble notched leaves
of ancestors, giving emblematic
grace to their persistence.

The leaves are last year's, the trees,
last century's. Young before
the Civil War, they screened a drive
along the levee, bore up the soft
night when twilight settled over
the river. Sold, transplanted half
a mile, they have grown wise watching
plantations cut, and shotgun houses
line side by side. Now, the grandeur
gone, they canopy their losses
like a monument, and fill windowsills
with coins of an outdated currency.

In this burgeoning there is no room
for regrets; I must cut down
three strong saplings by the house
and pull a dozen tiny oaks, riches
unneeded, near the azaleas. When
a hundred lives in me have come
to rock, the seedy earth gestures
with largess, "This too, this too."
So much is expendable, even beauty,
or the captors of the light; you
can call nothing home, except
the passage of the great and small,

leaves burning in the heart's land.

Landscape with Peasants

No chasm; no rise in the foreground
where a plowman pauses amid furrows;
nor, for a backdrop, the Alpine peaks
which Brueghel imposed on his Flemish
countryside. Instead, spread out
between bayous, flat rows of cotton
in bloom, and the Millet forms of men
with a hoe. An indolent sun idles
above pines, as the afternoon steams.
Admire how the very fields give off
nostalgia, their patchwork lines nearer
to art than use; caught in the alluvium
of change, the laborers, wearing red
bandanas and real overalls, still sweat,
beyond the reach of rhetoric—while we
are but spectators, out of the frame,
having, God knows, no hands for picking
cotton, seeing this as picturesque. Do
the figures bend now, or is it our
motion that gives them life? Beyond,
the levee ribbons green along the river,
where cargoes from other worlds pass
by, then out of the painting, leaving
the scene anchored to its past. A crow
caws from the gibbet of an electric pole;
what survives as we drive on is formal,
effort turning to beauty in the mind.

History

Shall we say this to the nameless
of history: Beyond that line of firs,
spring plantings ripen to bounty;
row by row the sheaved wheat bends
west of the barn; outlander birds,
billeted in an aspen grove, feast
on plenty. That is the scene, summer
order.

    Even the early windfalls
of the peach trees remain firm;
cumulus clouds practice identities.
When our eyes reach for the fields,
and seize the sky with a swallow's
sovereignty, all is as if: one might
affirm endurance.

             —What if the dead
reply that such contentment can make
no sense, much less justice (chance,
not poetry, concluding the human
fable), each summer but a pointless
denouement? One lives as one loves—
unreasonably, envying the stars' design,
where we may be, at best, a metaphor.

Route 29

i

It curved below the house,
like the last plow tracks
where a hill rises—
but always level with my mind.
Along with Amherst County farmers
going to Faulconer's General Store,
used cars being towed tandem
southwards, and behemoth trucks,
I rode it every day,
and again a hundred times
from my windows at night, before
dreams, in the hollow hours worse
than sleep, watching the lights
round the bends of my mind.

ii

Dorothy Faulconer who lived
downstairs told me how one night
she had lost her headlights,
driving down from Charlottesville,
and how a trucker, beams
on high, followed her all the way,
lighting her from behind.
Often I could feel
the dark room expand
about me and the fields beyond,
into a dizzy sea;
and then the beacon of a late car
below would cross my wall,
and the bed found its keel again.

iii

As the hills flushed red,
flowing into an idea of other
autumns, sometimes I thought back
toward the similarities of time,
and the child at the center.
Where the roads crossed,
I would remember the conjunctions
of love; but Valley winds
would drive the diverse

clouds down the Ridge, and climbing
the switchbacks through the gap,
I foresaw a thousand miles
of flight; my lives dispersed
like scattered birds.

iv

The mountains watch, flawless,
coeval with no one; we
are movement, marked like an edge
of road crumbling after winter's
bite. Half-knowing the denouement,
I still drive those curves
in dreams; they are my wise serpent,
uncoiling in the past, part
of the arc of time—never joining
with tomorrow as I ride forwards—
since all revelation is revision,
figures in a rear-view mirror—
never the meaning coming,
never the connection, the return.

Assateague in Winter

Half-adrift off the peninsula, it surfaced
to an ashen dawn and snow-driving wind,
casting leafless yardarms into the clouds;
the bridge from Chincoteague hung frail
as it rode out December. Driving to anger's
impulses, we paused. From the salt marshes

blue herons flushed, and through the mist
the wild ponies clustered, waiting roundup,
brown and motionless as cypress clumps.
The naked beach bled gray under our feet;
gulls, screaming, circled up, then lit
farther on, abandoning the carcass of a fish

nearly picked clean. Not a quarrel
but could be laid to rest there (cold
hands nestling close as birds) between
the desolation of the sempiternal sea
and the barren flank of dunes. Perhaps
—years and half a continent away—it is

the chill rain dripping through a pine,
fog huddling near the fields, that waken
longing; I scavenge through the bones
of the brittle past, the wingless ghosts,
where neither quarrels nor reconciliations
last, but only wind, cutting, cutting.

Abiding Winter

Abiding winter, here on this shortest day
whose light barely slices into the cold
and listening to the winds of memory,
I see days banked ahead like clouds, gray
into endless gray. Such muteness of earth
at the late year! All might be abandoned,
save where a scattering of sparrows feeds

silently, turning the last seed of fall
into their brief warmth. Perhaps a child
is playing somewhere now; perhaps a child
is playing in my mind, too pale for me
to see the face, humming a carol I cannot
hear. The rituals of the past are thin
as the arc of the sun that edges down above

the pines; nothing lies between my father's
death and me, except the vacuity of time—
the years gone, the transparent years to come.
Out by the graves, snow must be driving
over the range, futilely plowing emptiness,
while the stock wait it out in a draw. Gusts,
loosened now, shell the air, and a branch

crackles; reason at the wane could crack
too, or fly away with the startled birds,
or perhaps endure another year. At last,
suspended all the bloodless day, evening
gathers in the trees, curtaining cold for
tomorrow. The house remains dark. Abiding
winter is, not yet, but soon, abiding death.

Augusta County: Perspectives in Snow

Call it the first deep snow, December
settling in, a vision. If I imagined
herald flecks—the only light to reach
a sky of slag—who caught me in a dance
and turned my body into theirs: passage,
movement, brief and immaterial as breath,
well, by noon at Afton, crystals left
quick windshield rivulets, for tears,

and the pavement shone with the silver
of old mirrors. And now, with afternoon
drawing its blinds, a million mica bits
have thickened, like a sauce, and laid
their mineral glaze over rock and trees;
every sound and motion, every prospect
of the dipping road will be transformed,
and I remind myself, "You think you know

the Valley, her classic fields, but that
is in the past, with yesterday's drive,
last night's dream." This steady scrim
will not be outrun: the crunch of tires
moves with my mind, my feet will founder
in it soon. I remember my father, years
ago, clearing the path, and trying then
to conjure his in music's measured sadness,

and consider what has changed. Time works
like that: after being long in coming,
suddenly it takes hold, things congeal
at its center, and we are in it—we *are*
it—so that the old regrets and fears,
even a consuming quarrel, seem distant
now as the dark, expressive hills of fall
that journey quietly in winter's company.

In the Adirondacks

For Daniel and Barbara

Well, we have arrived, our wits
cleared by the long drive
of all but the immediate. As luck
would have it, everything's awash;
what presences we might have entertained
of lake and prospect hills infolding
vanish in a monochrome of clouds
and grayed-out distances. That rain

can claim the landscape from our senses
bears, perhaps, its own intelligence;
but ours prefers a neat
and brilliant noon, lines that predicate
our possibilities. At nightfall,
fireflies and—opposite—
pale constellations in Vermont, but not
a single star to breach the alien

fields. The shore resists desire,
the trees and grass, the one
intrusive road too low and sodden
for our voices to take hold; we hang up
hats and coats and yellow boots,
and tune ourselves instead to Beethoven's
quartets, Prokofiev by Barbara's hands—
devising formal apprehensions

of the darkness.—Writing this tonight,
I measure the economy of shadow,
which reveals the luminous within,
surpassing light's harmonics. Now, a low
and vibrant wind like music
rises from the silence, summoning
the hills we could not see,
the dazzling water, noumenal and blue.

Islands

Islands! They skim along the continent
like birds, pecking
at the coast, then winging out, wind-
drawn, to sea. The solstice
takes their soundings, marking the depths
with brilliant paint. A wooded shore
turns suddenly to cove and sand;
the anchor drops bayside, where sheets
are tacking into motion
and an insect in the bougainvillea vine
whistles as the stranger walks by.
On board again, departure is in order.

ii

The water scans my sleep; I dream
a song that is the song of the world,
as if immense arms held
this narrow berth. We waken then,
enclosed by an embrace of islands, coral-
rimmed, and the sea stained
cobalt blue. Poincianas! royal palms!
the port quickens in your shade;
on the beach, the figure of a perfect
shell, lustrous under the thumb,
murmurs from its rosy mouth
a sonorous salutation without a name.

iii

On St. John, you have been netting fish,
little fish, you say,
now all back in the sea. The wind
tosses our hair into fronds;
wisps of foam toboggan on the waves.
I cannot go farther than this
into understanding: all is immediate,
brilliance and visible motion,
there for the taking; yet a darkness inside
keener than light will not
be stilled, but paces in its cage,
brooding on its masks and its conundrums.

iv

I am in the eye of the white cockatoo
who reigns over Ardastra Gardens:
the saucer leaves of sea grape
fanning the green fruit ("Sour, sweet—
you have to taste to know")—
a traveler's palm in feathered headdress,
flamingos prancing. Listen,
white cockatoo: in the ululation
of the wind, I hear what is coming:
glory along the sea roads,
and the islands feeding in my hand,
before they take their flight toward dusk.

Birds at Night

Birds at night are nearly still, pinioned
by shadow; but sometimes islands of sound
shape when a cardinal calls as if in dream
and branches move with the weight of love,
or the bluejays chatter suddenly, shredding

the garden. In the dark nest of the house
I am awake, waiting as the hours wheel
like skimmers, watching my daughter, draped
in white, sail through sleep. A warbler's
note catches the swell of the wind, rides;

the curtains blow, wings spread within me,
and I am carried, my child following, over
the branched bodies, to plains of space
where the arc of giant wingspans shines
the night long. The earth has disappeared,

but a few forms climb to join me; it is they,
the night birds, brilliant now; singing
surrounds me, and we soar toward dawn
together, drawn on by the dazzling child
who rises at the center, higher, beckoning.

Strawberries

I saw their cousins in the woods last week,
globes of desire among the poison oak;
prey for some nimble quadruped, perhaps,
who since has nibbled at them tidily,
they tempted me with summer's sweetest shapes,

more succulent for pleasing but the eye.
Now, juice from these domestic berries stains
the bowl, as slices fall under the knife,
and leaves and stems become discarded stars.
Their breeding rounded firm in ruddiness,

these are the tastiest, surely, of their kind,
crushed between spoon and palate. Let us eat
such fruits, beauty in glass—but I recall
the nestling plants, sunlight at play on leaves,
that feast of fire in the wilderness.

Grass

A stream of grass ripples across
the marsh; the loam
is yeasty as bread. Somewhere
a thrasher finds particular release
in three notes, high, repeated. There,
a trampled clump shows its roots,
while by my hand a hundred shoots
push upward toward the humming plane
where insects turn. All effort seems
uneven next to this perdurable peace,
smooth as water, where the light arrives
identically; below reflection lies
the undivided quietude of dreams.
A green worm mounts a blade, thin
as breath; cutting from its flock,
a bird dips near. Something in my mind
loosens, as the wind,
carrying the single leaf, the cries,
waves past. So grass will grow
each summer, erupting from the grain
of dark. Grow, grow through rock,
the way love revives
among the igneous signs of loss;
grow through me now, that I may know
what it is to be all otherness,
when desire has come home
and my body has become the land again.

Watching Bees

Rippling down the screen of an open
window, the Rosa-Montana vine hums
like the strings when a bass player
finishes his solo. It is the bees
I listen to each morning, dressing
after coffee. They must be working
first the middle tangles. Through

the bedroom, mellow light thickens
to their buzzing. There! Crossing
each other's paths, they appear now
in the sun, hovering on the farther
stems, alighting—then back in shade,
taking shortcuts for the blossoms
on the other side. Down the cascade

of leaves, every instant is activity:
pink clusters tremble, and a branch
is shaken to the tendrils. As green
as shoots in spring, a lizard weaves
along the vine, then stops—a single
stillness. His little belly is a body,
like the bees', sensing things. God,

are they vulnerable! The gardener's
shears, a gale—and they are gone,
with their hunger and their husbandry.
Strange that I should feel connected
to their lines of purpose. Heaven knows,
even though I'm stepping out today,
I won't return with nectar—nothing

so delicious, so unmixed; but simply
thinking that they can preserve what
is only, for the rest of us, perfume,
is sweet; it will keep the bees and me
together if a frost arrives, to know
they can survive on garnered glories,
salvaging something of our innocence.

Crows

The crows stir up the darkness with their wings,
proceeding west; a stand of cedars mutes
their drifting cries, which last as if a hand
had gestured to design a word, then left

the meaning in the air. Black into black,
they disappear now. Even in the mind,
something about their form remains opaque;
I cannot penetrate to their idea,

remote behind that stern, deliberate rise,
the wholeness of their flight. The commonest
eludes us most. Among the folds of hills,
the corn will leap up, flaming in the wind,

as summer runs; when the crows come again
in waves above the quincunxes of green,
what will it matter then that alien wings
have just descended over me like death?

Variations at Pass Christian

i

For the lucidities of summer, lawns
and pleasantries are not mirrors
enough: you need the sea, rippling
freely as it multiplies the light
and turns it into motion. The way
it shimmers sometimes seems to fit
the mind; today—sounding its long
undifferentiated note, and ruffling
its pigeon-mottled skin—it listens
only to itself, dreaming—as birds,
shaping the wind, allow nothing
alien in their sufficient flight.

ii

But the net of reflection reaches
even among the indistinguishable.
Doubly shaded (parasol, and glasses
darker than this morning's storm),
you watch the ocean arch its back;
working over the furrows, you pluck
a wave, reel it in until it washes
itself out, then cast again, mood
and sea in confluence. By the rim,
figures move—a ghostly language,
riding to the limits of the world,
and taking on the body of the light.

iii

If truth rose suddenly, Minerva
bursting from the seamless blue,
it would have many heads, and some
might be surprising. What a farce,
were rationality merely our desire,
an inner music calling into dark,
discordant space. And if Descartes
were here, reasoning by the waves
winnowed in sun, would he recognize
the beat, and say it was the same
as his old Lowland sea, the surf
still sounding in the mind of God?

iv

A fanfare sounds to the west, as if
a blinded man were playing chords,
remembering. Trimming the ragged
sea edge, gulls do their prospecting
while a girl whistles her way along
the shores of evening. The vision
does not endure; but it will be good
sailing after dark, tacking across
the Sound, when ship and water match,
as the sheets groan under the riddle
wind, shifting around and taking us,
reconciled, toward a strange release.

Peaches

i

Cobblers, pies, preserves, salads, peaches
and cream—even a pulpy ice:
since a spring without a freeze
turned early blossoms into this surfeit
of fruit, we have eaten peaches
every way we know, not forgetting
right from the branch, fuzz barely washed
under the faucet. Take one, now,
from the bowl, a world ripe
with the continents of summer's color.

ii

Long, unwrinkled days lead to evenings
nearly as long, and cooler, when phoebes
describe arcs around the trellises,
and rising flycatchers belie the stillness
of the air. Today we picked some more,
filling old-fashioned jars
with juice and golden flesh—gathering too
a little weariness, but sweet,
as after playing with a child
or singing late to friendship's music.

iii

After the immoderate midday sun,
my father was shade, measure,
and perspective. If one pail of peaches
was brought in on a summer's afternoon,
it was enough for him, knotting
the different threads of need and pleasure.
This fruit preserved is husbanding happiness
for future weeks; something of autumn
is already in their ripening,
the reconciliation of reason and love.

iv

The clean and candid light of Spanish rooms,
a simple love affair in summer clothes—
both quick and beautiful,
these call for ceremonial, like fruit
served on a blue-willow plate. Is this not

funereal, finally—the unnamed seed
of dying in even the freshest peach,
and all our rituals the savoring
of ourselves, most perishable,
but delighting in what resembles us?

Magpies

Tending their tree, they are—
clearing the brittle twigs, plucking
off berries, then giving the air
a good crisp call—
not the songbirds' cheer,
but a celebrant's plainchant tone,
or the cluck of a housewife

with no time for dulcet note. In
a round, they rise
to the crest, return,
feed by the frugal roots, on the bib
left by the morning's snow,
as clean as the magpies'
breast, under their priestly

black. Working, they heed the body,
but mind the spirit's
order too, which kneads
without measure wisdom's bread,
and sees past scattered
grain, to wings unnumbered
arching over distant fields of light.

Apples

They are not evil, merely beautiful,
a likeness of the heart—or so thought Eve,
it seems (although she might have meant to pick
a plum, a peach). The Greeks agreed, and thus
began a war. Surely the wicked queen

and William Tell both knew they stood for fate;
even Sir Isaac's science triumphed in
their awful fall. As for Cézanne, who saw
himself under their guise, he put their truth
in paint: the shape, the light, the way an eye,

caught by a bowl of fruit, reflects their shine,
or as their roundness signifies the hand,
as firm and ample as a woman's breast.
Consider these, the image of desire:
their russet mirrors autumn afternoons,

the sound of horns in Mozart, trees in flame.
The knife is next. They glisten, halved, the juice
transpiring on the lobes; the polished seeds
are scattered; then the palate understands
the joy of apple, with the cracking skin,

the crisp and mellow flesh, which must, consumed,
become the body that we love the most.
There will be little left: the stubborn core,
a stem—the trophies of the tongue's delight,
the evidence of death devoured again.

Buck Moths

Suddenly, they eclosed from everywhere,
the late year's scarlet-banded
offering, blooming
skyward. Males flying first,
they were searching out their dream, spun
from a worm (the females
quivering on the oaks, or huddled, sticky,
in the mulch). Quick beauty
hovered on their routes, before, starving,

they showered down,
and struggled, body heaving still, wings
inscribing flight on stone. The last
ones dying, winter descended
like a swoon. Too natural.
They were born into the garden
of deceit, where sly mortality
presides, and sows
a hecatomb of membranes, the futile lifting

of a final wing. Now the casual
wind, leaf-surfeited,
scatters its trophies under a dark moon,
circling toward another year;
the flame is gone,
and the earth hardens into stone,
before such a munificence of creatures
cast aside—the prodigality
of a jaded prince, brooding among his jewels.

Eating Pears at Midnight

The others are mostly asleep, the child
wrapped close to her original peace; alone
in the kitchen, I treat myself to gourmandise,
seasoned with a feeling of nostalgia.

All the windows open onto an October night,
mild, where a pale light dips in pools left
from the evening rain, and the honeysuckles
still bloom over the fence. How sweet

the air, and then the juicy autumn pear,
purloined from myself and tomorrow's salad,
enjoyed in stealth as a silent companion—
making insomnia delicious. On the porch,

the dog, half-blind, whines from old age,
his seventeen years weightier than my own
thirty-seven. Thinking forth, I cannot guess
what I shall know on the same edge of ruin,

later—but could wish it like this night,
a solitude to be made use of, a wakefulness
that calls the senses out from their dull
custom, to taste a full, ripe fruit;

then memory will feast, with the rosy
peeling falling around, bruises cut out,
one's dark self as company, and time
like a telescope pulling down the stars.

Destin: Swimming on Easter Day

Vindicating the early sun, torsos
bob beyond the parasols;
bodies turn, heliotropes following the girls
that flower from the sandy
runes—flanks bared, patches of color
hoisted like fanions. The gulls

dividing up their field of blue,
the leaves of surf unfolding—motion here
is all subsumed to light, the scene
as still and close-knit
as a painting. Confirming sundry winds,
a few sunfish tack out

among the blades of sea. Such purpose
suits the day. After a hundred
strokes: a taste of salt,
the sandbar, and another view—
the breakers filled, the shore consumed
in white. The wholeness

scatters briefly, then comes back.
What holds the harmony
is gesture, the coherent act, as in a ritual,
of fitting body and belief—
the waves and swimmer
joined, pleasure sounding the world

like a shell. The text is words of water,
words of light. Below, the constant
rhythm. For a moment,
diving marries dream and vision.
With every stroke the darkness yields.
I think you understand what I mean.